Contents

You can find words shown in bold, **like this,** in the Glossary.

What is water?

Water is a **natural** material. Water is a **liquid**. It flows down streams and rivers and fills the seas and oceans. The surface of the Earth is covered with more water than land.

Water is refreshing to drink. You need to drink water every day to stay alive. Other animals need to drink water, too. Plants also need water to live.

The properties of water

Rainwater is called **fresh** water.
So is water that comes out of
a tap. It has no smell or taste.
Water is **transparent**. You
can see right through it!

When you stir sugar into water, the sugar seems to disappear. This is called **dissolving**. Sea water has salt dissolved in it. That is why it tastes salty.

Ice and steam

The water you drink is a **liquid**. But water can be a **solid** too. Ice is solid water. Water turns to ice when it gets very cold. This is called freezing.

Water can also be a **gas**. Steam is
water in gas form. Water turns to
steam when it gets very hot. This is
called boiling.

Clouds and rain

Clouds are made up of millions of tiny drops of water. This water comes from the sea. It turns into a **gas**, making the air damp. When the gas cools down, it turns back into drops of water.

When the drops of water in a cloud get heavy, they fall as rain. Some rain soaks into the ground. Some flows into streams and rivers, and then back to the sea.

Finding water

We need lots of water for drinking and washing. Some of our water comes from huge lakes called **reservoirs**. A reservoir is made by building a wall called a **dam** across a river.

There is water inside rocks under the ground. A deep hole called a well is dug into the ground. The water is pumped up from the bottom of the well.

Water to your home

Water flows to your house along pipes. There are big water pipes under roads and streets. Smaller pipes carry the water to taps in your home.

In many parts of the world people do not have water taps in their houses. They often have to walk many kilometres to a well to get water.

Drinking water

Your body cannot work without water.
An adult needs to drink about 2 litres
of water a day to stay healthy. That's
two large drink bottles full!

Bottled water is water that comes from a spring. A spring is a hole in the ground where water comes out. The water contains **chemicals** called minerals that are good for you.

Water for plants

Plants need water to live and grow.
They suck up water from the soil
through their roots. Outdoors,
plants get water from rain.
You have to water plants
that live indoors.

Some plants live where it is very hot and dry. Cactus plants live in the desert, where it only rains once or twice a year. A cactus stores water in its stems.

Washing with water

Water is good for washing. This is because it picks up dirt and carries it away. Hot water washes things better than cold water.

Water cannot wash away oil or
grease on its own. You have to use
soap, washing-up liquid or washing
powder too. These pick up the oil or
grease and the water washes it away.

Water power

We can use flowing water to make things work. At a water mill, rushing water from a river hits a water wheel. It makes the wheel turn. This works machines inside the mill.

Water is also used to make electricity. Water is stored in a huge **reservoir** behind this **dam**. It rushes down big pipes and works machines that make the electricity.

Cleaning water

Dirty water from washing and flushing the toilet must be cleaned. It goes down a waste pipe from the sink or the toilet. Then it goes into a big, underground pipe called a **sewer**.

The sewer carries the dirty water to a **sewage** works. Here the water is cleaned using special **chemicals**. Then the clean water flows into a river or into the sea.

Water pollution

In some places, people throw rubbish into rivers and seas, making them dirty. **Poisonous chemicals** flow in from factories. This is called **pollution**.

Sometimes dirty water from towns is not cleaned before it flows into the sea. If swimmers or surfers swallow the water, it can make them very sick.

Fact file

▶ Water is a **natural** material.

▶ **Fresh** water has no smell and no taste.

▶ Sea water tastes salty.

▶ Water is **transparent**, which means you can see right through it.

▶ The water you drink is a **liquid**.

▶ Water can also be a **solid**, called ice, and a **gas**, called steam.

▶ Water lets some electricity flow through it.

▶ Water is not attracted by magnets.

Would you believe it?

Ice is water which has frozen solid. If all the ice in the world melted, the sea level would rise by several metres. This would drown low-lying islands and towns near the coast.

Glossary

chemicals special materials that are used in factories and homes to do many jobs, including cleaning

dam strong wall built across a river. The water from the river makes a lake behind the dam.

dissolving mixing something with water so that it disappears into the water

fresh water that is clean and does not smell or taste of anything

gas substance like air that completely fills any container in which it is kept

liquid something that flows, such as water and oil

natural comes from plants, animals or rocks in the Earth

poisonous something that makes a person or animal ill

pollution rubbish or poisonous chemicals that are thrown on to the ground, or into the air, rivers and seas

reservoir lake made by storing water from a river. Most reservoirs are made by building a dam across a river.

sewer huge underground pipe that carries dirty water to a sewage works

sewage dirty water from homes and factories

solid something which has a definite shape

transparent see-through

More books to read

Images: Materials and Their Properties
Big Book Compilation
Heinemann Library, 1999

It's Science! Water
Sally Hewitt
Franklin Watts, 2001

My World of Science: Water
Angela Royston
Heinemann Library, 2001

Science All Around Me: Materials
Karen Bryant-Mole
Heinemann Library, 1996

Water is a Solid, Liquid and Gas
Bobbie Neate
Longman, 2001

Index